SandCastle

Healthy Habits

Taking Care of Your Teeth

Mary Elizabeth Salzmann

Consulting Editor, Diane Craig, M.A./Reading Specialist

Publishing Company

Published by ABDO Publishing Company, 4940 Viking Drive, Edina, Minnesota 55435.

Copyright © 2004 by Abdo Consulting Group, Inc. International copyrights reserved in all countries. No part of this book may be reproduced in any form without written permission from the publisher. SandCastle™ is a trademark and logo of ABDO Publishing Company.

Printed in the United States.

Credits
Edited by: Pam Price
Curriculum Coordinator: Nancy Tuminelly
Cover and Interior Design and Production: Mighty Media
Photo Credits: BananaStock Ltd., Corbis Images, Digital Vision, Eyewire Images, Rubberball Productions

Library of Congress Cataloging-in-Publication Data

Salzmann, Mary Elizabeth, 1968-
　　Taking care of your teeth / Mary Elizabeth Salzmann.
　　　　p. cm. -- (Healthy habits)
　　Includes index.
　　Summary: Explains in simple language the importance of taking care of one's teeth.
　　ISBN 1-59197-554-9
　　　　1. Teeth--Care and hygiene--Juvenile literature. [1. Teeth--Care and hygiene.] I. Title.
RK61.S16 2004
617.6'01--dc22
　　　　　　　　　　　　　　　　　　　　　　　　　　　　　　　2003057793

SandCastle™ books are created by a professional team of educators, reading specialists, and content developers around five essential components that include phonemic awareness, phonics, vocabulary, text comprehension, and fluency. All books are written, reviewed, and leveled for guided reading, early intervention reading, and Accelerated Reader® programs and designed for use in shared, guided, and independent reading and writing activities to support a balanced approach to literacy instruction.

Let Us Know

After reading the book, SandCastle would like you to tell us your stories about reading. What is your favorite page? Was there something hard that you needed help with? Share the ups and downs of learning to read. We want to hear from you! To get posted on the ABDO Publishing Company Web site, send us e-mail at:

sandcastle@abdopub.com

SandCastle Level: Transitional

Taking care of your teeth is a healthy habit.

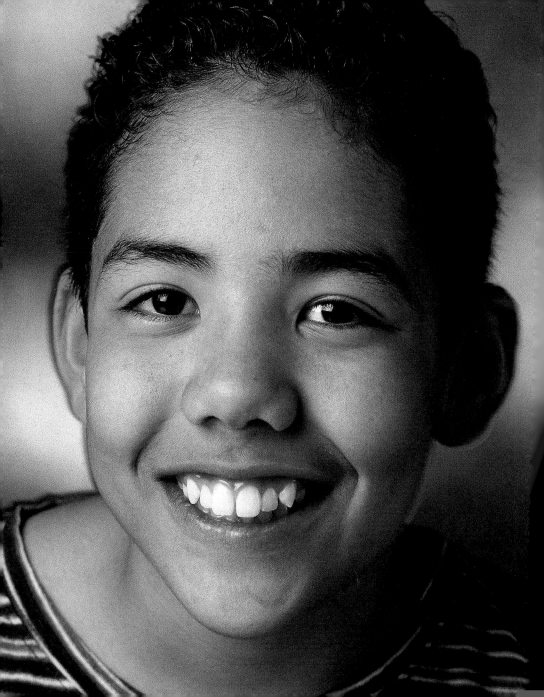

Taking care of your teeth helps prevent cavities and gum disease.

Taking care of your teeth means brushing them every day.

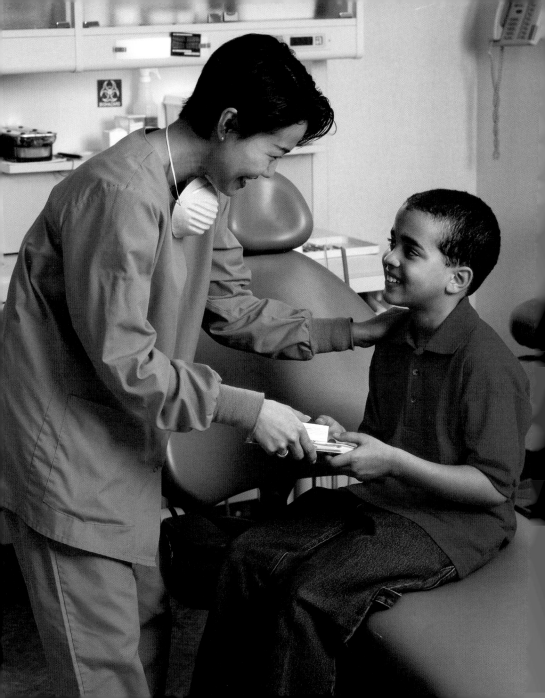

Taking care of your teeth means going to the dentist.

Rachel has braces on her teeth to straighten them.

Peter and his dad brush their teeth together.

The dentist shows Diane an X-ray of her teeth.

Ned looks at himself in the tiny dentist's mirror.

Erin learns the right way
to brush her teeth.

How do you take care of your teeth?

Did You Know?

A full set of baby teeth is 20 teeth. A full set of permanent teeth is 32 teeth, including 4 wisdom teeth.

There are four different kinds of teeth: incisors, canines, premolars, and molars.

Toothbrushes were first developed in China around 1500. The bristles were made from natural bristles such as pig, horse, and badger hair.

Paul Revere was a dentist.

Glossary

braces. wires and brackets attached to the teeth to straighten them

cavity. a hole in a tooth caused by decay

dentist. a person trained to help people take care of their teeth

gum. the pink flesh that surrounds the base of the teeth

habit. a behavior done so often that it becomes automatic

healthy. preserving the wellness of body, mind, or spirit

X-ray. an invisible beam of light; a photograph of the inside of the body taken with an X-ray

About SandCastle™

A professional team of educators, reading specialists, and content developers created the SandCastle™ series to support young readers as they develop reading skills and strategies and increase their general knowledge. The SandCastle™ series has four levels that correspond to early literacy development in young children. The levels are provided to help teachers and parents select the appropriate books for young readers.

Emerging Readers
(no flags)

Beginning Readers
(1 flag)

Transitional Readers
(2 flags)

Fluent Readers
(3 flags)

These levels are meant only as a guide. All levels are subject to change.

ABDO
Publishing Company

To see a complete list of SandCastle™ books and other nonfiction titles from ABDO Publishing Company, visit **www.abdopub.com** or contact us at:

4940 Viking Drive, Edina, Minnesota 55435 • 1-800-800-1312 • fax: 1-952-831-1632